Airdrie

D0789151

·ANIMALS ILLUSTRATED·

Polar Bear

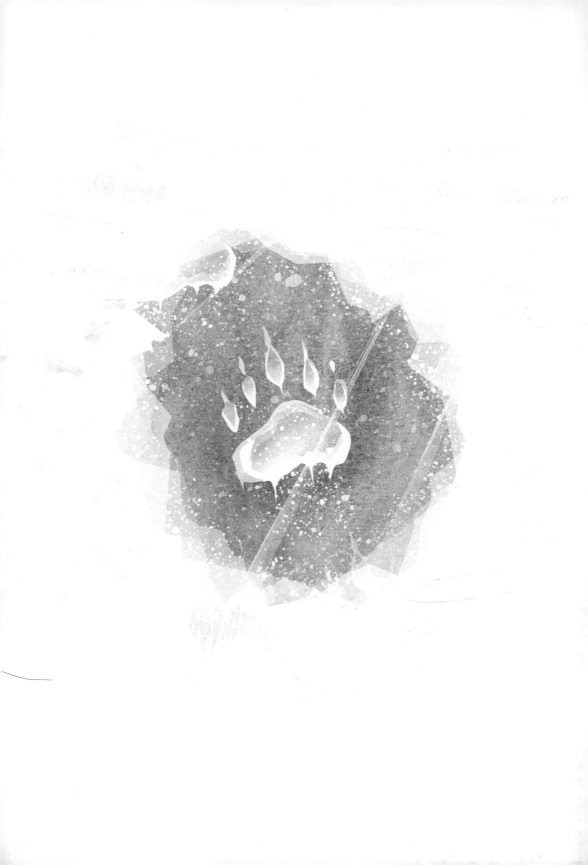

·ANIMALS ILLUSTRATED·

Polar Bear

by **William Flaherty** • illustrated by **Danny Christopher**

111 · 601 Main Street S
Airdrie, Alberta, T4B 3G3

INHABIT
MEDIA

Published by Inhabit Media Inc.
www.inhabitmedia.com

Inhabit Media Inc. (Iqaluit), P.O. Box 11125, Iqaluit, Nunavut, X0A 1H0 · (Toronto), 191 Eglinton Avenue East, Suite 301, Toronto, Ontario, M4P 1K1

Design and layout copyright © 2016 Inhabit Media Inc.
Text copyright © 2016 by William Flaherty
Illustrations by Danny Christopher copyright © 2016 Inhabit Media Inc.

Editors: Neil Christopher, Kelly Ward
Art Director: Danny Christopher

All rights reserved. The use of any part of this publication reproduced, transmitted in any form or by any means, electronic, mechanical, photocopying, recording, or otherwise, or stored in a retrievable system, without written consent of the publisher, is an infringement of copyright law.

We acknowledge the support of the Canada Council for the Arts for our publishing program.

This project was made possible in part by the Government of Canada.

978-1-77227-079-2

Printed in Canada

Library and Archives Canada Cataloguing in Publication

Flaherty, William, 1965-, author
Polar bear / by William Flaherty ; illustrated by Danny Christopher.

(Animals illustrated)
ISBN 978-1-77227-079-2 (hardback)

1. Polar bear--Juvenile literature. I. Christopher, Danny, illustrator
II. Title. III. Series: Animals illustrated

QL737.C27F53 2016   j599.786   C2016-905443-8

Table of Contents

The Polar Bear

The polar bear is a huge bear that lives in the Arctic. Polar bears weigh between 880 and 1,543 pounds (399 to 699 kilograms). Male polar bears can be twice as big as females.

Polar bears look very different from other types of bears. Their fur appears white for most of their lives, though it yellows as they get older. Their bodies are also longer and sleeker than other types of bears. In the wild, polar bears usually live about 15 to 18 years, but scientists have found some bears in the wild over 30 years old!

Polar bears are bold, powerful, and surpisingly fast.

Let's learn more about polar bears!

Range

Polar bears stay in the Arctic all year round. They do not leave the Arctic in the cold winter months like other animals do. They do, however, travel great distances in search of food.

Most bears are land animals, but polar bears are unique! They live on the land, the sea ice, and in open water.

Polar bears are very adaptable. In the summer months,
they can be found on land and along the shoreline.
During the winter they can travel great distances out
onto the sea ice, and they use the sea ice to hunt from.

Skeleton

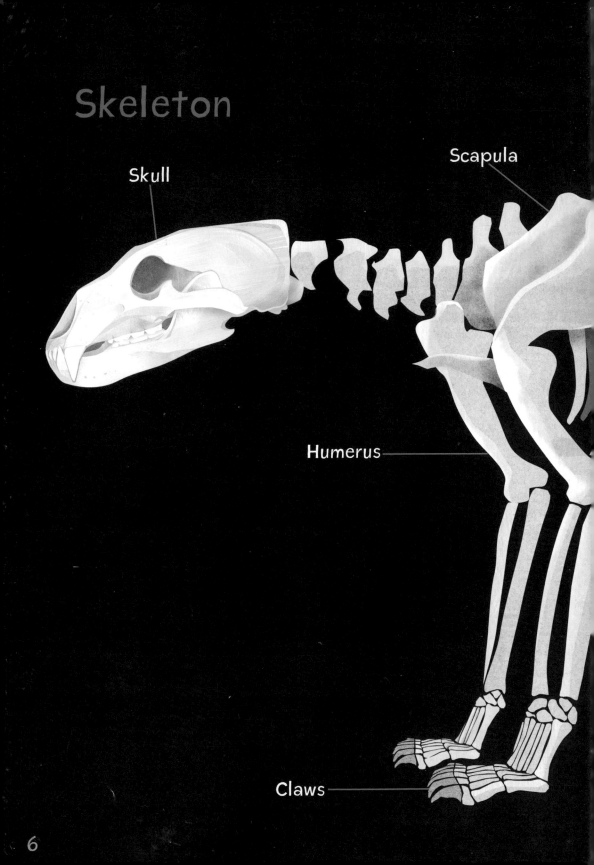

Skull

Scapula

Humerus

Claws

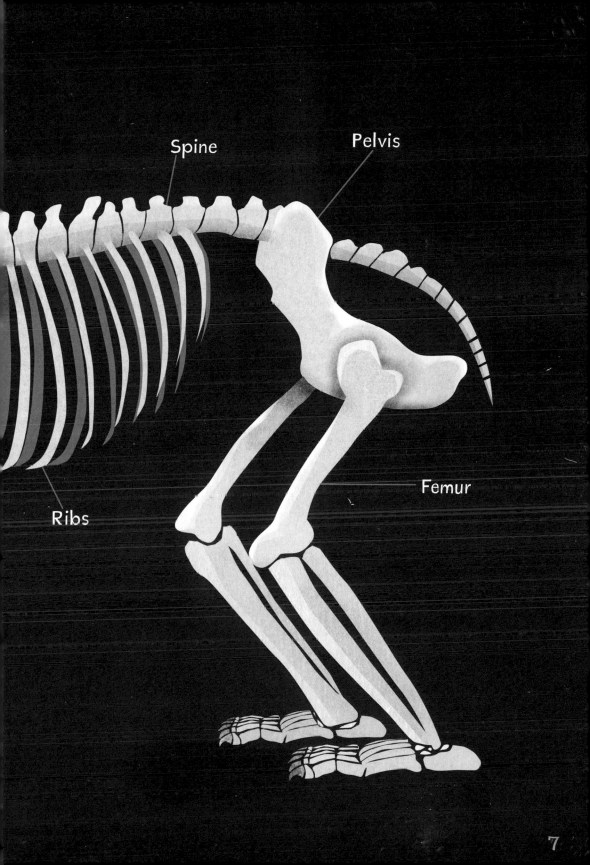

Spine

Pelvis

Femur

Ribs

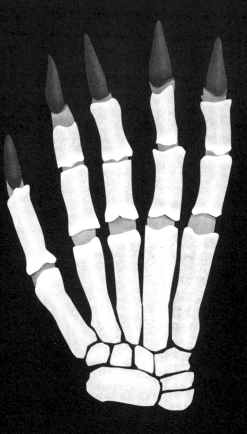

Polar bear paws are very large. Large paws help polar bears to walk on snow by spreading out their weight over a larger area. When the bears are swimming, the large paws act like paddles to help them move through the water quickly. Polar bears use only their front paws to swim.

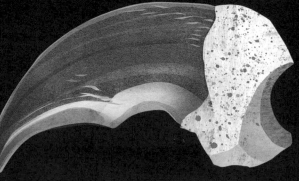

Claw (actual size)

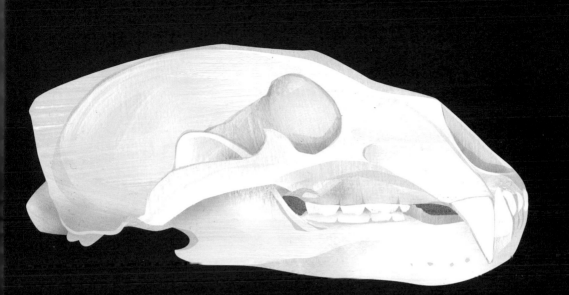

Polar bears have a very sleek and narrow skull. Their narrow heads help them to cut through the water as they swim after seals to eat. Their jaws are very powerful and contain 42 very sharp teeth.

Canine Tooth

Diet

The polar bear is a carnivore. That means it eats meat. It is the largest carnivore in the world that lives on land.

Polar bears mainly eat seals. They will also eat walrus, muskox, caribou, bird eggs, and small rodents—if they can catch them! Polar bears will also eat berries and seaweed when they can find them.

Polar bears will even hunt beluga whales and narwhals when they become trapped in cracks in the sea ice. Polar bears are near the top of the Arctic food chain. That means that they can hunt most animals in the Arctic!

Babies

Baby polar bears are called "cubs." Cubs are born between November and January in dens dug by their mothers. Usually two cubs are born, but sometimes three cubs are born. They leave the den in March or April, as the weather warms up. The whole time they are in the den, the cubs have only their mother's milk to eat.

Hunter

Polar bears catch seals in the winter by waiting patiently at holes in the sea ice that seals use to breathe. Bears wait silently at these breathing holes for hours waiting for a seal to appear. In the Arctic, the ocean is covered in ice during the winter, spring, and late fall, so bears hunt at breathing holes during all these seasons.

During summer, when there is open water on the ocean, seals float on top of the water while they sleep. A bear will swim up to a sleeping seal, very quietly, and catch it! This is an easy way for bears to catch a good meal. Bears can also sneak up on seals that are resting on ice floes and catch them from below.

Polar bears hunt very patiently and carefully, just like human hunters. They are very quiet, and they check their surroundings to decide the best way to sneak up on their prey.

Swimmer

Polar bears are fantastic swimmers. They can swim great distances, and they also dive underwater for up to three minutes at a time. In the Arctic, polar bears are often seen swimming in deep open water, far away from land.

A bear was once tracked swimming more than 400 miles (643 kilometres) on a nine-day journey!

Fun Facts

Looking at a polar bear, you would assume its fur is white, right? Actually, the hair of the polar bear is transparent, meaning it has no colour at all. Polar bear hair is also hollow. This colourless, hollow fur allows the sun to pass through the bear's hair and warm its skin, keeping it warm in the cold Arctic. The skin of the polar bear warms up very quickly because it is actually black!

The bear's hollow fur also holds air, which helps these heavy bears float while they swim!

The biggest polar bear ever caught was found in Kotzebue Sound, Alaska. It stood 11 feet tall (3.4 metres) and weighed 2,200 pounds (998 kilograms)!

3.4 m	11 ft
3.1 m	10 ft
2.7 m	9 ft
2.4 m	8 ft
2.1 m	7 ft
1.8 m	6 ft
1.5 m	5 ft
1.2 m	4 ft
0.9 m	3 ft
0.6 m	2 ft
0.3 m	1 ft

Nanurluk

In Inuit mythology, there are many stories of giants—giant people and giant animals! Stories are told about a type of giant polar bear called a "nanurluk." The nanurluk is huge (bigger than an iceberg!) and its hair is often said to be covered in thick ice.

William Flaherty is a conservation officer and an avid hunter who regularly volunteers with Iqaluit Search and Rescue. He lives in Iqaluit, Nunavut.

Danny Christopher is an illustrator who has travelled throughout the Canadian Arctic as an instructor for Nunavut Arctic College. He is the illustrator of *The Legend of the Fog* and *A Children's Guide to Arctic Birds*. His work on *The Legend of the Fog* was nominated for the Amelia Frances Howard-Gibbon Illustration Award. He lives in Toronto with his wife and three children.